Animals vs. Humans

SNAKES STRIKE

Kathleen Reitmann

WWW.APEXEDITIONS.COM

Apex is distributed by North Star Editions:
sales@northstareditions.com | 888-417-0195

Produced for Apex by Red Line Editorial.

Photographs ©: Shutterstock Images, cover, 1, 4–5, 10–11, 14–15, 18–19, 20–21, 22–23, 26–27, 28–29, 30–31, 32–33, 34–35, 36–37, 38–39, 40–41, 42–43, 44–45, 46–47, 56–57; Dr. Sellers/Grady Hospital/CDC, 6–7; Hulton Archive/Getty Images, 8–9; ANT Photo Library/Science Source, 12–13; James Gathany/CDC, 17; Per-Anders Pettersson/Getty Images News/Getty Images, 24–25; iStockphoto, 49, 54–55; Thomas Coex/AFP/Getty Images, 50–51; Matt Hunt/SOPA Images/Sipa USA/AP Images, 52–53; Red Line Editorial, 58–59

Library of Congress Control Number: 2023922211

ISBN
979-8-89250-213-9 (hardcover)
979-8-89250-234-4 (paperback)
979-8-89250-275-7 (ebook pdf)
979-8-89250-255-9 (hosted ebook)

Printed in the United States of America
Mankato, MN
082024

NOTE TO PARENTS AND EDUCATORS

Apex books are designed to build literacy skills in striving readers. Exciting, high-interest content attracts and holds readers' attention. The text is carefully leveled to allow students to achieve success quickly.

TABLE OF CONTENTS

Chapter 1

RATTLESNAKE ATTACK

A rattlesnake shakes its rattles. It warns a hiker to stay away. But the hiker treads too close. The snake lunges and bites her leg. Venom shoots into her bloodstream.

Rattlesnakes often coil their bodies before they strike.

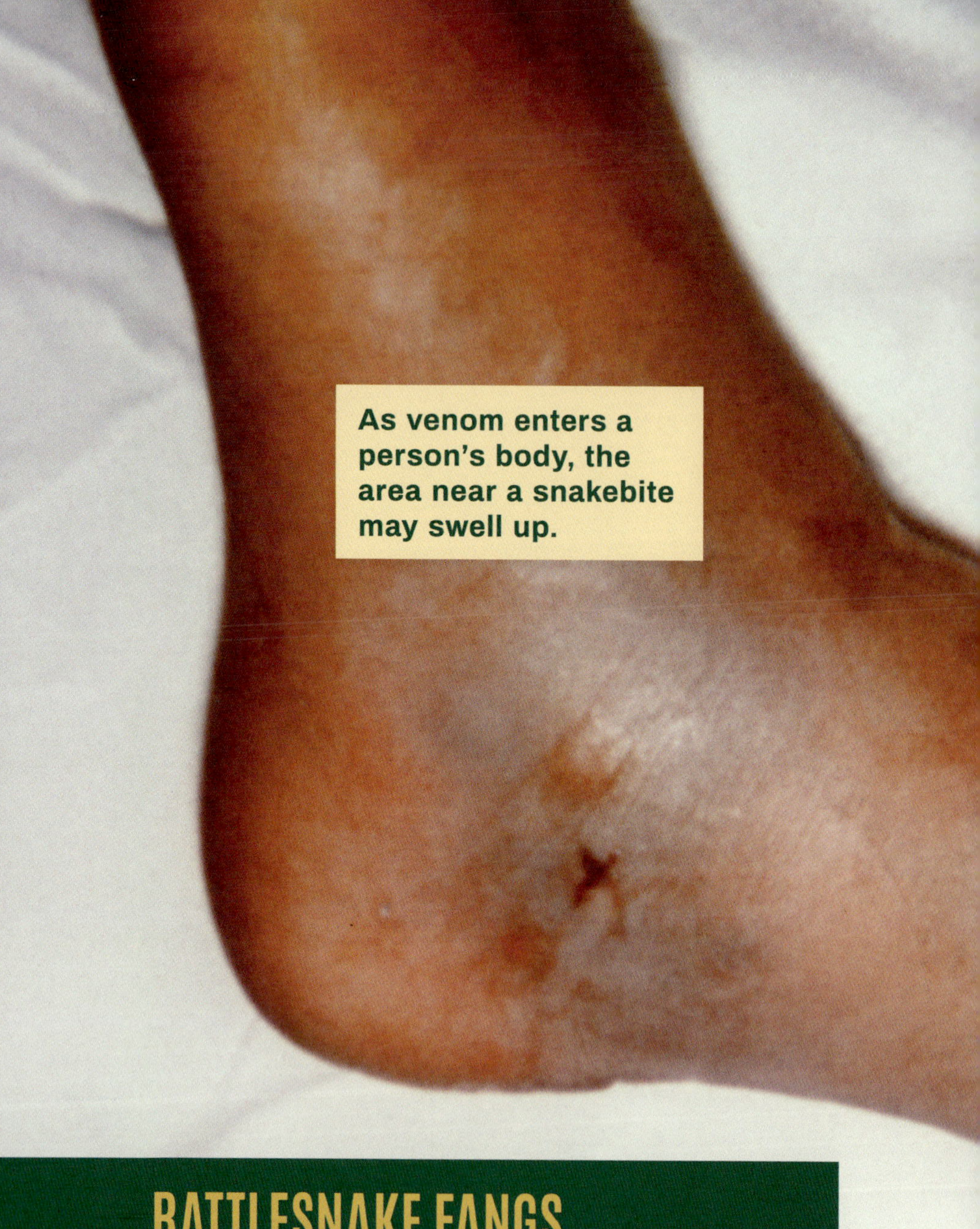

As venom enters a person's body, the area near a snakebite may swell up.

RATTLESNAKE FANGS

A rattlesnake's fangs can grow 6 inches (15 cm) long. The fangs usually lie flat. But they stand up when the snake strikes. Venom shoots through them.

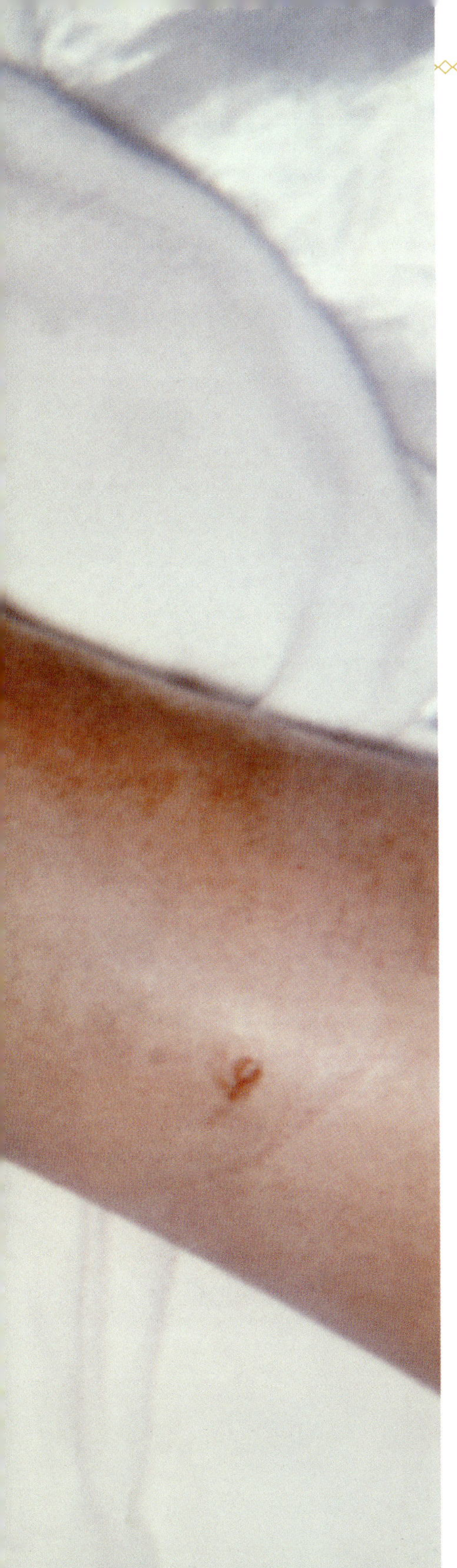

The hiker tries to stay calm. She knows the venom will spread faster if she panics. She calls 911.

Soon, she feels dizzy and weak. Her leg swells. Will help get there fast enough?

The hiker hears sirens. An ambulance arrives. Health care workers give the hiker medicine. It stops the pain.

At the hospital, the hiker gets antivenom. It treats her bite. She feels better. Luckily, she got help in time.

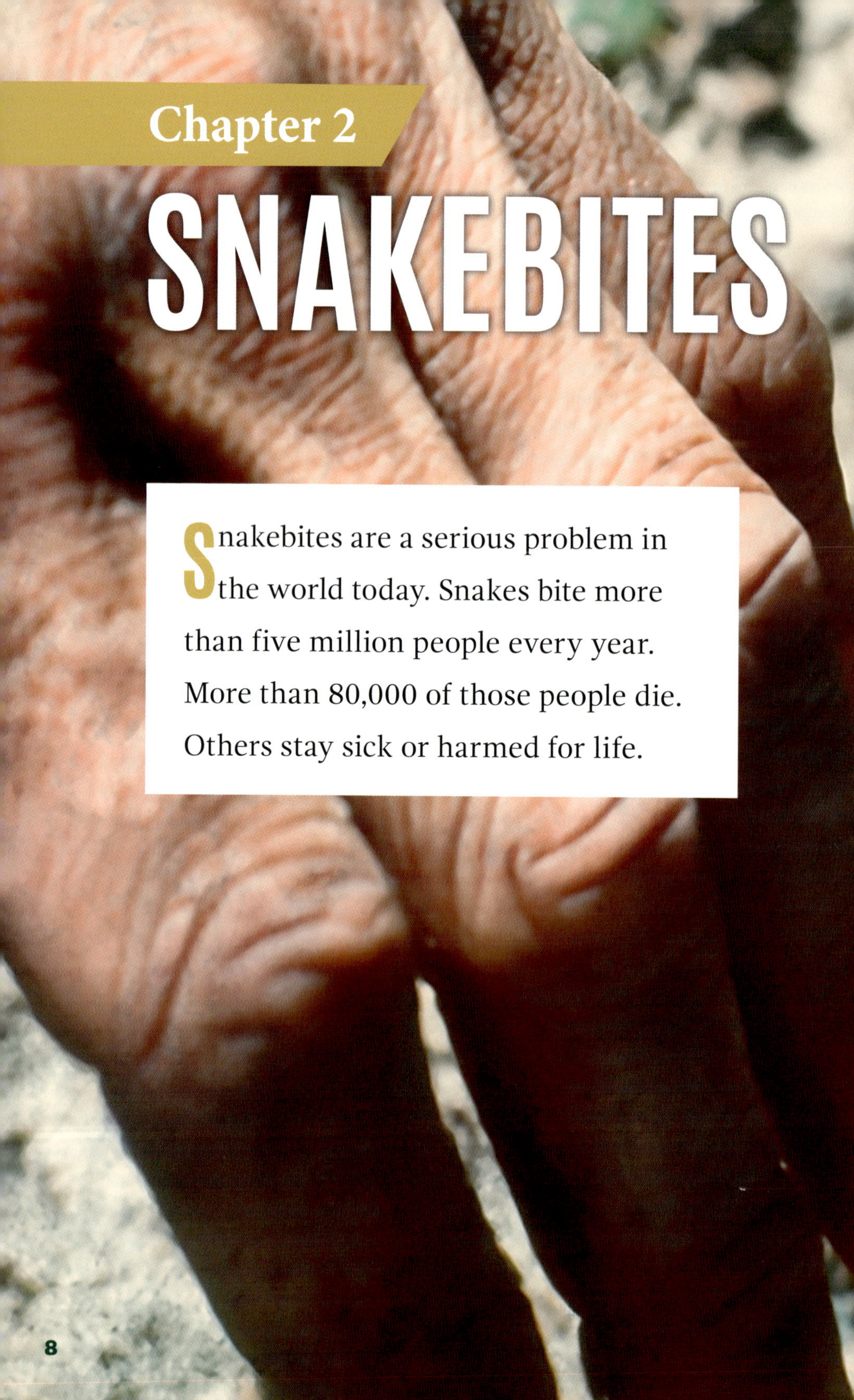

Chapter 2

SNAKEBITES

Snakebites are a serious problem in the world today. Snakes bite more than five million people every year. More than 80,000 of those people die. Others stay sick or harmed for life.

Sidewinders live in the US Southwest and northwestern Mexico. Bites from these snakes are rare.

Snakes don't look for people to attack. But people often go where snakes live. For example, many snakes live in fields where farmers dig. Farmers come across them by accident. The snakes get scared. They strike to defend themselves.

SAW-SCALED VIPERS

Saw-scaled vipers are a group of venomous snakes. They live across Africa, the Middle East, and Asia. Saw-scaled vipers are tiny. But they are aggressive. Their bites kill more people every year than any other type of snake.

Saw-scaled vipers rub their scales together when they are afraid. This makes a hissing sound.

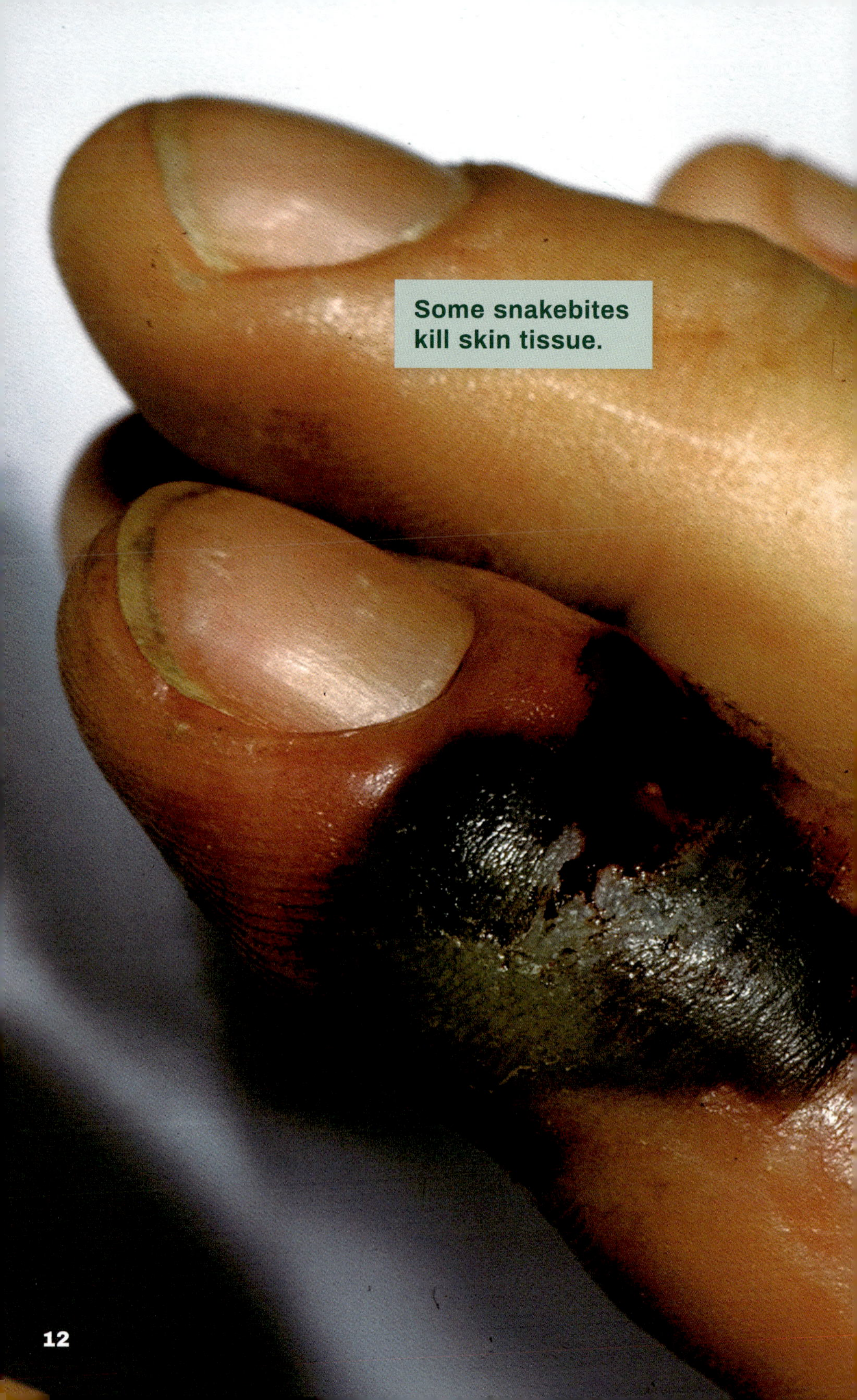

Some snakebites kill skin tissue.

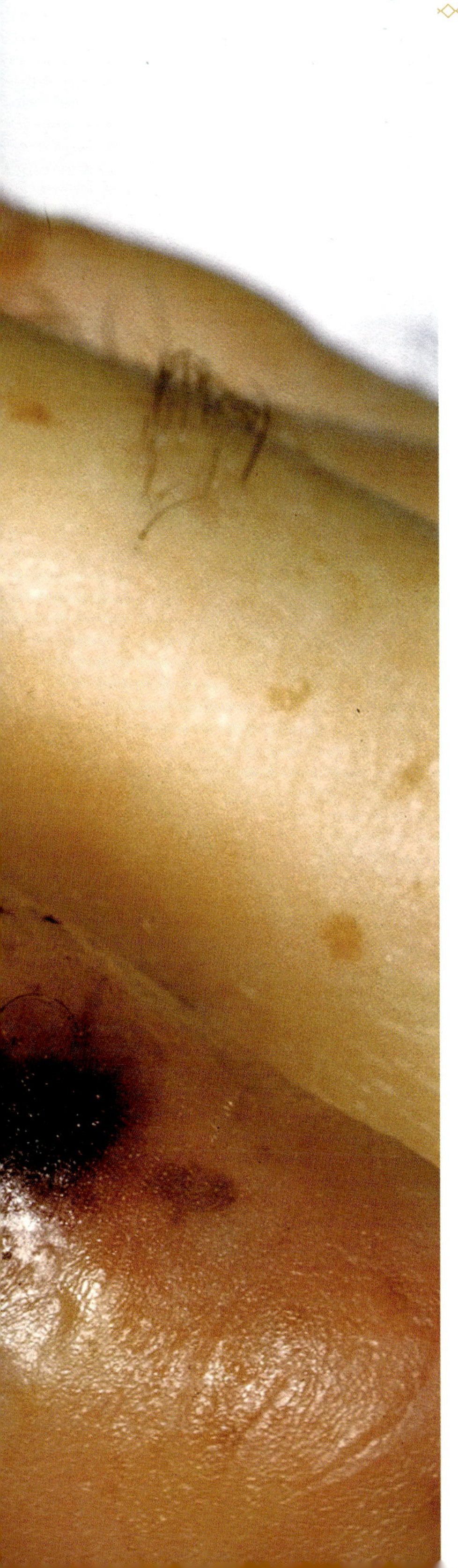

Snakebites are often painful. They cause swelling and redness. Other harm depends on the type of snake. Vipers are one type. Their bites can lead to heart attacks. Vipers can also cause bleeding inside people's bodies.

Elapids are another type of snake. They include cobras, mambas, and taipans. Their venom tends to attack the nervous system. It paralyzes muscles. This can make it hard to breathe. It can also stop the heart from beating.

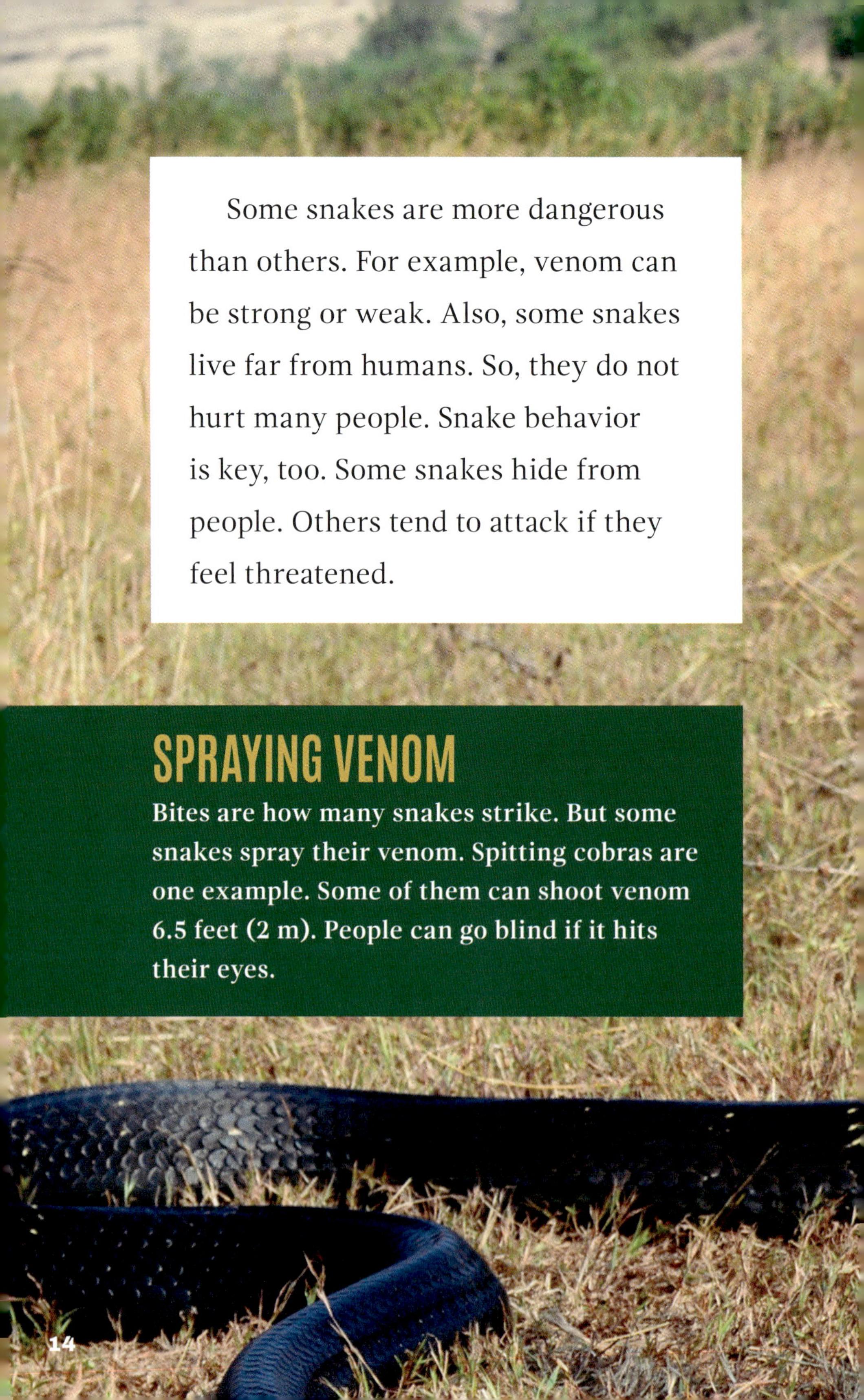

Some snakes are more dangerous than others. For example, venom can be strong or weak. Also, some snakes live far from humans. So, they do not hurt many people. Snake behavior is key, too. Some snakes hide from people. Others tend to attack if they feel threatened.

SPRAYING VENOM

Bites are how many snakes strike. But some snakes spray their venom. Spitting cobras are one example. Some of them can shoot venom 6.5 feet (2 m). People can go blind if it hits their eyes.

The king cobra releases lots of venom into its victim. One strike can kill a person in minutes.

That's Wild!

SNAKE IN THE STROLLER

Snakes love to hide. A family in Tennessee learned this fact the hard way. The parents went for a walk. Their baby rode in a stroller. After the walk, they put the stroller in the garage. But the couple didn't close the garage door. Later, there was a surprise. They found a copperhead in the stroller. The snake was in the baby's blankets. It tried to strike the father. But he jumped back in time.

The couple felt shocked. But they were glad that their baby wasn't in the stroller at the time.

Copperheads live throughout the eastern half of the United States.

Chapter 3

SNAKES IN AFRICA

Snakes are a danger in many parts of Africa. They are especially harmful south of the Sahara Desert. Snakes kill more than 20,000 people there every year. The puff adder is one of the deadliest. It's also one of the most widespread.

The puff adder's fangs bite deep. Sometimes it doesn't need venom to kill its prey.

The puff adder is a type of viper. Vipers cause harm across Africa. But their venom takes days to kill people. Other snakes' venom works faster. Mambas and cobras are two examples. Their venom kills in just hours.

BLACK MAMBAS

The black mamba is very deadly. Two drops of venom from this snake will kill a person. The snake bites many times when it attacks. Black mambas are fast, too. They can travel 12 miles per hour (19 km/h).

The black mamba is a large snake. It can grow up to 14 feet (4 m) long.

Farmers in Africa are most at risk of snakebites. They often work barefoot. Or they wear sandals. Snakes often hide in fields or under rocks. They can bite farmers' feet. Farms also tend to be far from hospitals. So, it can take too long to get help.

CAMOUFLAGE

Many snakes use camouflage. They blend in with their surroundings. This helps them stay safe from predators. It also means people may not see them. People may step on or near a snake. Then they get bitten.

Gaboon vipers live in forests in western and central Africa. Their scales blend in with roots and leaves.

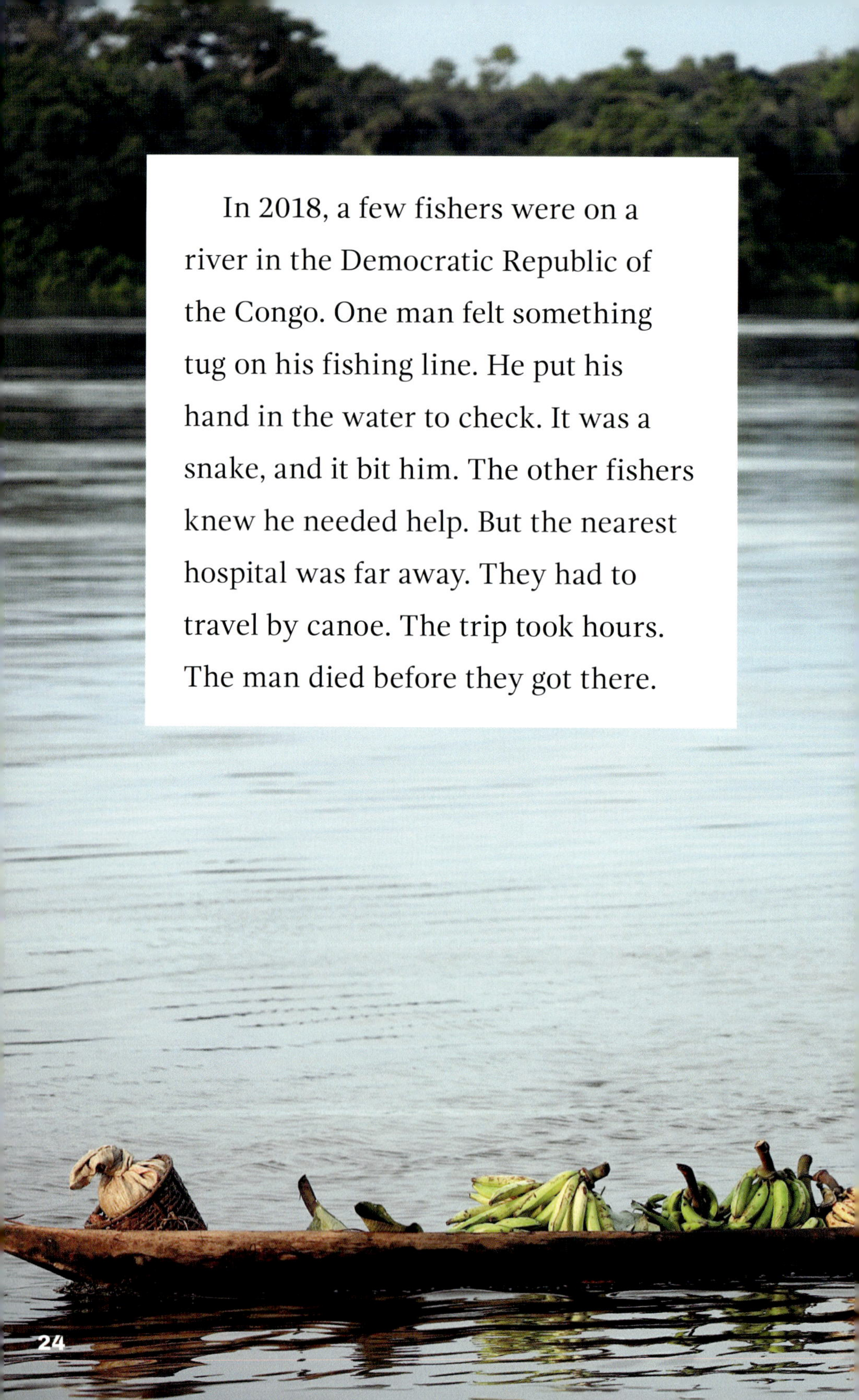

In 2018, a few fishers were on a river in the Democratic Republic of the Congo. One man felt something tug on his fishing line. He put his hand in the water to check. It was a snake, and it bit him. The other fishers knew he needed help. But the nearest hospital was far away. They had to travel by canoe. The trip took hours. The man died before they got there.

The Congo River, and the rivers flowing into it, are a key source of food for many people.

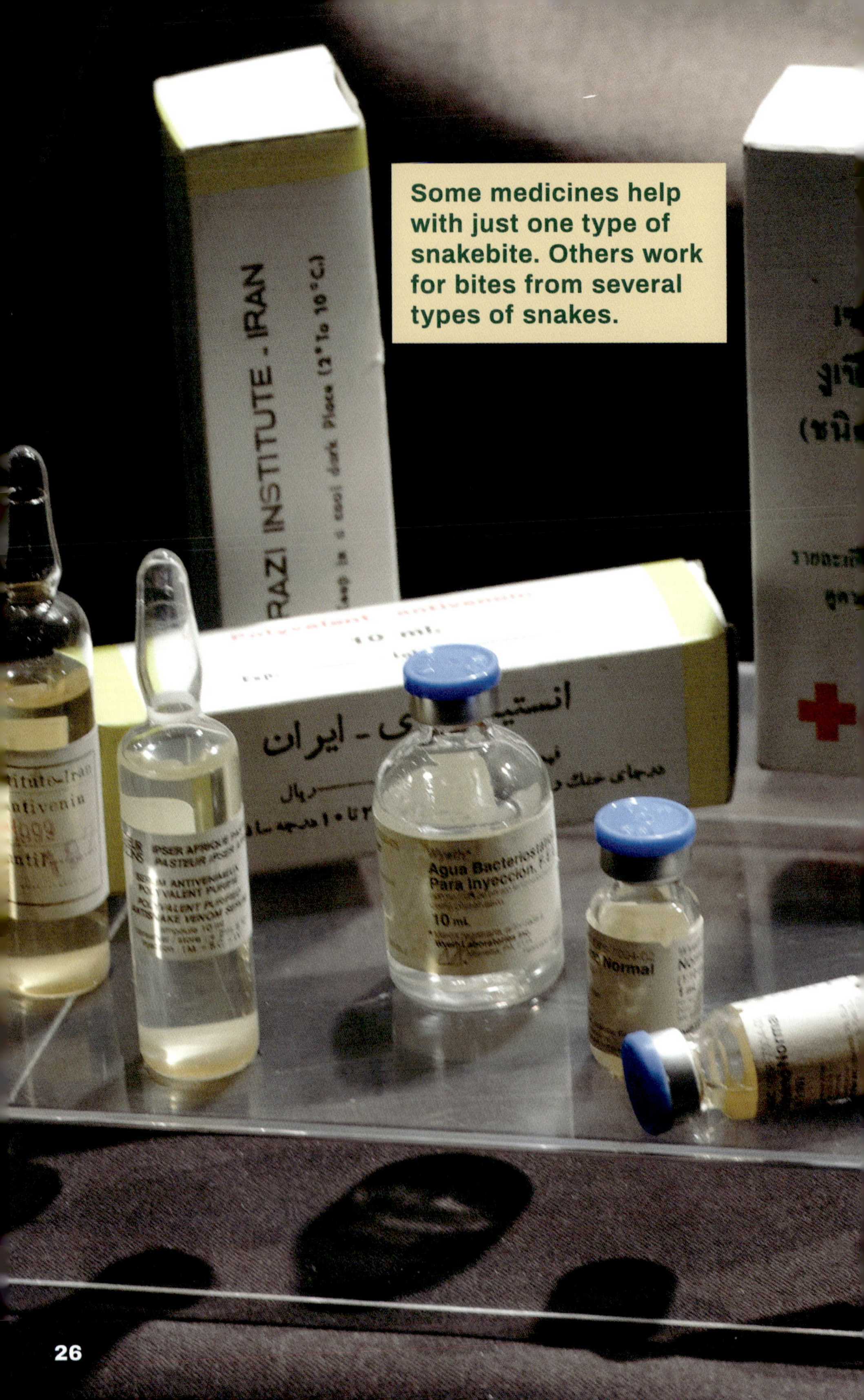

Some medicines help with just one type of snakebite. Others work for bites from several types of snakes.

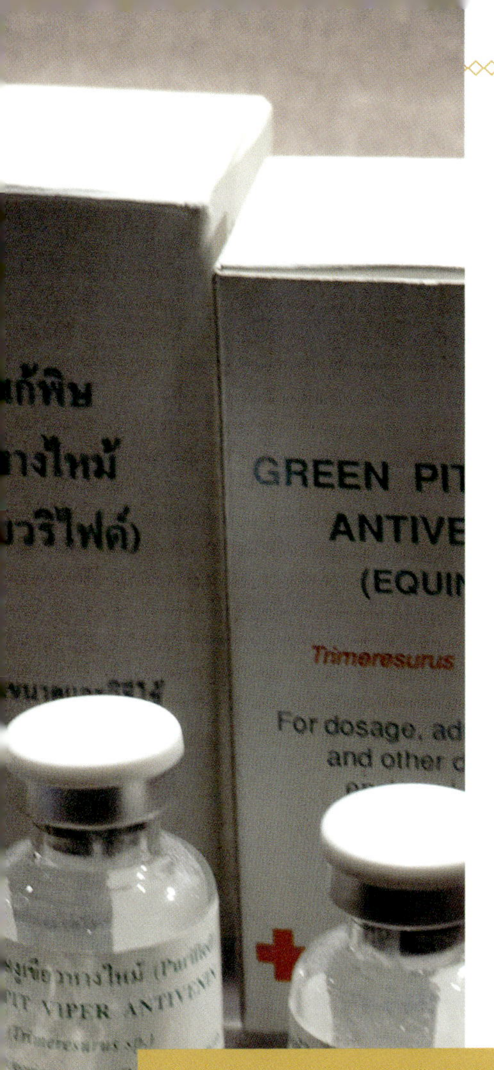

Treating snakebites can cost a lot of money. People often need several doses of medicine. Each dose can cost more than $100. So, some people try to make their own medicine. It is cheaper. But it doesn't work as well. It may be too weak to help.

MEDICINE SHORTAGE

In 2023, a snouted cobra bit a man in South Africa. Thankfully, he found doctors. But they didn't have any antivenom. The man began vomiting and soon couldn't walk. He faced extreme pain for hours. But he survived.

Chapter 4

SNAKES IN ASIA

People in Asia also battle snake attacks. Snakebites kill at least 100,000 people in Asia every year. About half those deaths happen in India. The Russell's viper is the biggest killer. It lives throughout most of India.

The Russell's viper mainly eats rodents, such as rats. But one bite has enough venom to kill a person.

Spectacled cobras are often 3.3 to 4.9 feet (1.0 to 1.5 m) long.

The Russell's viper kills more than 20,000 people in India each year. But India has other dangerous snakes. The spectacled cobra hisses a warning. Then it strikes. Its venom paralyzes. A bite can make people stop breathing. The common krait is active at night. It often bites people sleeping on the floor. A type of saw-scaled viper lives in India, too. These four snakes cause most snakebites in India. So, they are called the "Big Four."

Many bites happen during monsoon season in South Asia. At this time of year, lots of rain falls. So, many snakes come out of their holes. Monsoon season is also the time for harvest. Farmers are outside a lot. Many of them get bitten.

THE SIND KRAIT

The Sind krait lives in the Thar Desert. This desert crosses both India and Pakistan. The Sind krait is similar to the common krait. But its venom is even stronger. So, its bites are hard to treat. Victims need a special kind of antivenom.

In the early 2020s, nearly two billion people lived in South Asia. More than half of them worked in farming.

Snakebites are also a problem in parts of East Asia. For example, the many-banded krait lives in China. This snake rarely bites. But its venom is powerful. So, it's a top killer in China.

CHINESE COBRAS

Chinese cobras are found across southern China. Their bites aren't always deadly. But they kill tissue cells. As a result, bitten people often need surgery. This removes the dead tissue.

In China, many-banded kraits cause more than 25 percent of deaths from snakebites.

Deadly cobras live throughout Southeast Asia. Some live on land. Others live in water. These snakes are dangerous to fishers. For example, Malaysia has sea snakes. These snakes can get caught in fishing nets. Then they bite fishers. The bites don't hurt much. But the venom can kill people quickly.

PIT VIPERS

Southeast Asia is home to several deadly pit vipers. These snakes have pits between their eyes and nostrils. The pits sense heat. This helps the vipers find and strike their prey.

The white-lipped island pit viper lives in parts of Indonesia and Timor-Leste.

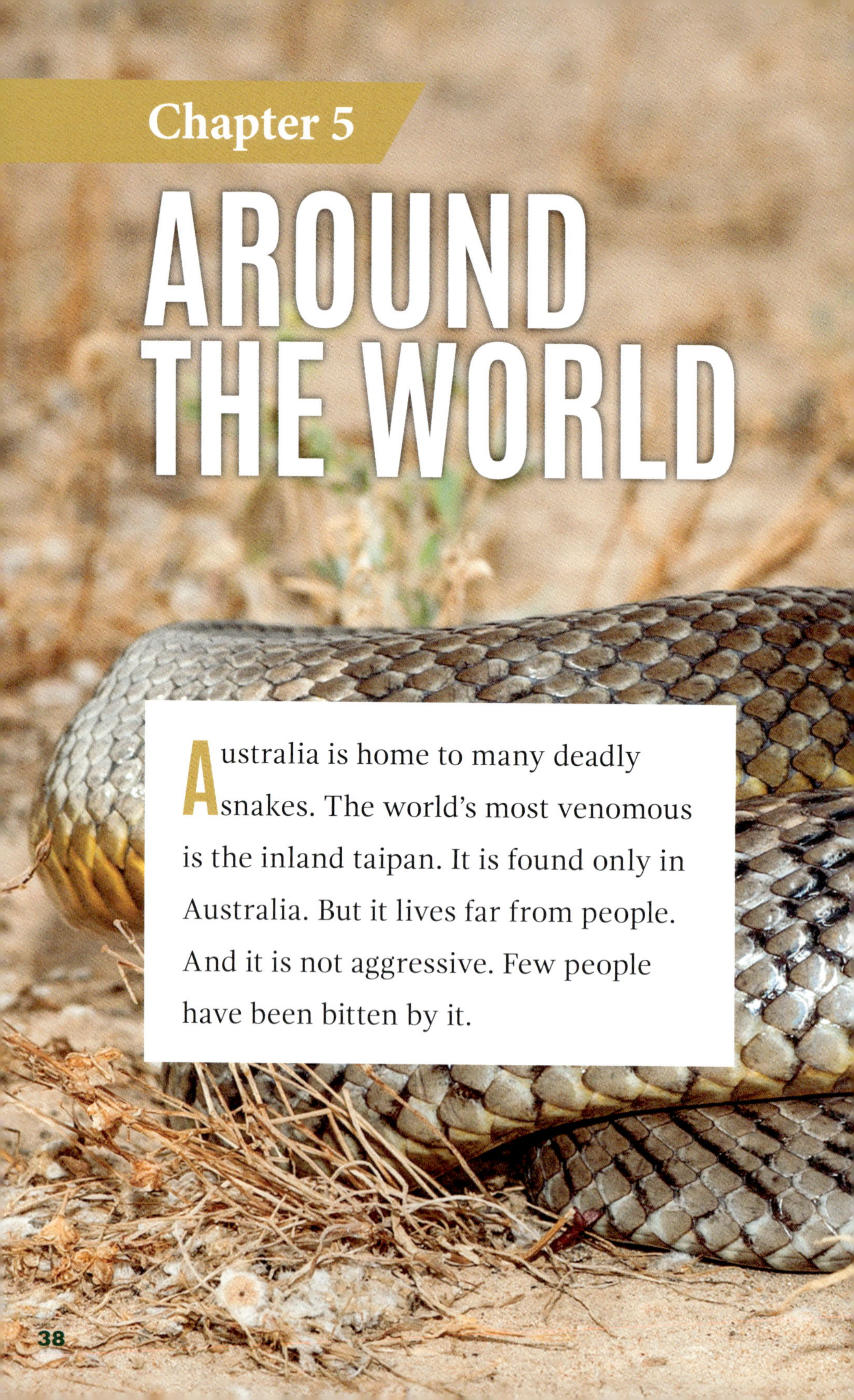

Chapter 5

AROUND THE WORLD

Australia is home to many deadly snakes. The world's most venomous is the inland taipan. It is found only in Australia. But it lives far from people. And it is not aggressive. Few people have been bitten by it.

The inland taipan's venom kills prey extremely quickly.

Many bites from eastern brown snakes happen when people try to kill the snakes.

Australia has strong health care systems. Most people can get antivenom quickly. So, snakes kill just a few people there every year. When people do die, the eastern brown snake is often to blame. This snake has small fangs. But its venom is incredibly strong. People must get help quickly to survive.

WESTERN BROWN SNAKES

Western brown snakes are similar to eastern brown snakes. Their venom is weaker. But each bite has much more venom in it. So, western browns can still cause great harm.

Tiger snakes live in Australia. They are responsible for many bites. Tiger snakes often live near people's homes. They mainly eat mice and small mammals. Tiger snakes come out at night. People don't see them. They can step on snakes by accident. Tiger snake venom causes severe pain. It tingles at first. Then the venom spreads. The victim has a hard time breathing.

Without treatment, about half of people bitten by tiger snakes die.

The fer-de-lance can grow up to 7 feet (2 m) in length.

In the Americas, pit vipers are the biggest threat. There are at least 50 types. The fer-de-lance is one of the most dangerous. This pit viper is large, quick, and aggressive. It is found throughout Central America and as far south as Peru. Some live in southern Mexico, too.

GREEN ANACONDAS

Green anacondas live in South America. These huge snakes can weigh hundreds of pounds. They don't use venom. Instead, they are constrictors. They kill by squeezing their prey. However, they rarely go after people.

In the United States, deadly snakebites are rare. Even so, many dangerous snakes live there. Water moccasins, copperheads, and rattlesnakes are a few examples. They bite thousands of people every year.

INVASIVE SNAKES

Many people buy and sell snakes from other countries. This market is big in the state of Florida. However, the snakes sometimes escape. They become invasive. The snakes go live in the wild. There, they harm native plants and animals. For example, anacondas and pythons are both problems in Florida.

Water moccasins often live in or near swamps.

That's Wild!

LOVE BITES

Some snake attacks are mistakes. The snakes don't mean to bite people. But they get confused. One example took place in Australia. Divers were swimming. They were at the Great Barrier Reef. The divers got some visitors. Some olive sea snakes appeared. These snakes can grow to be more than 6 feet (1.8 m) long. They have very strong venom.

Olive sea snakes rarely bite people. But this time, the sea snakes thought the divers were snakes, too. They tried to mate with the swimmers. They coiled around the divers' legs. Some even bit the divers. Thankfully, the divers survived.

Olive sea snakes are common off the northern coast of Australia.

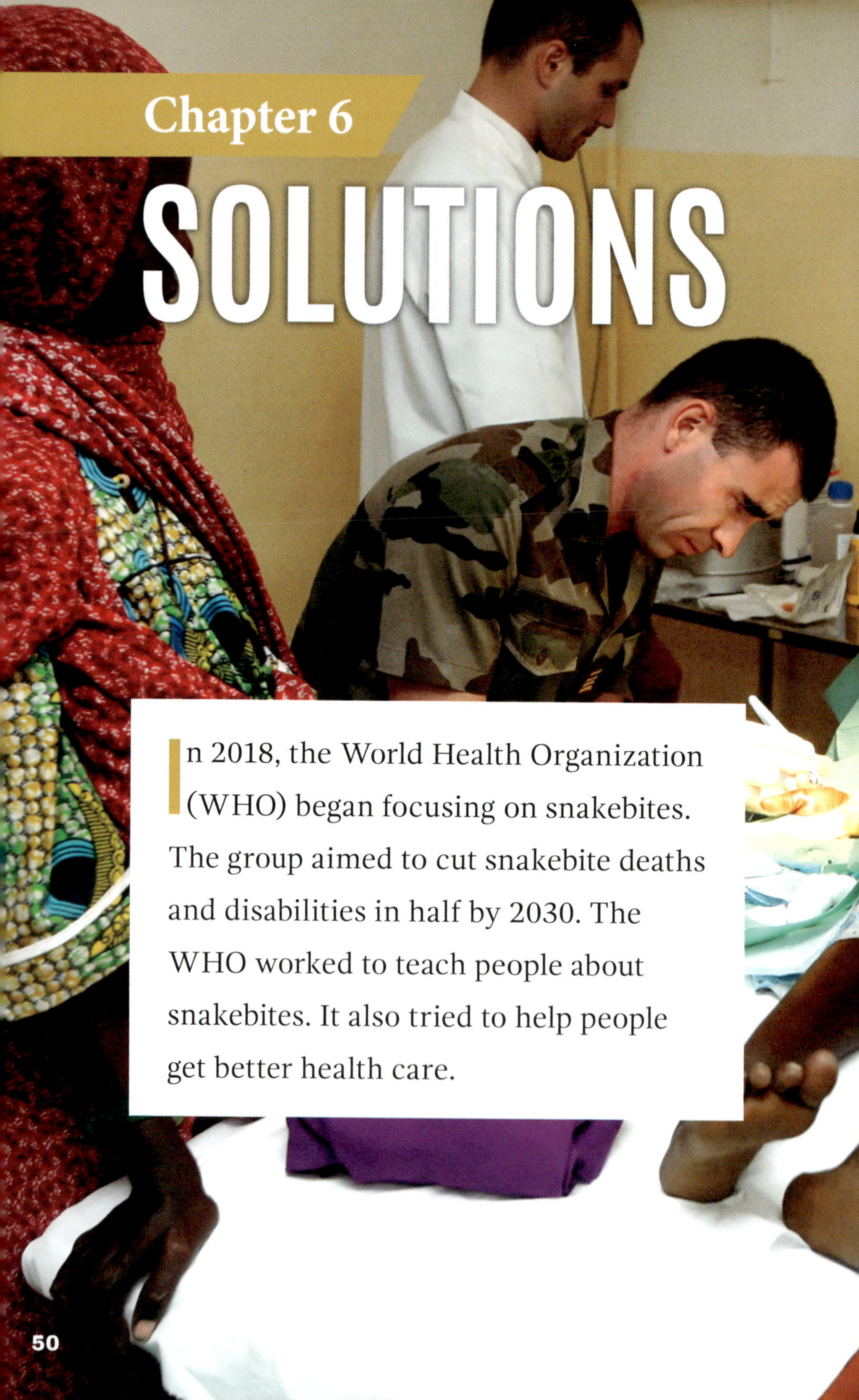

Chapter 6

SOLUTIONS

In 2018, the World Health Organization (WHO) began focusing on snakebites. The group aimed to cut snakebite deaths and disabilities in half by 2030. The WHO worked to teach people about snakebites. It also tried to help people get better health care.

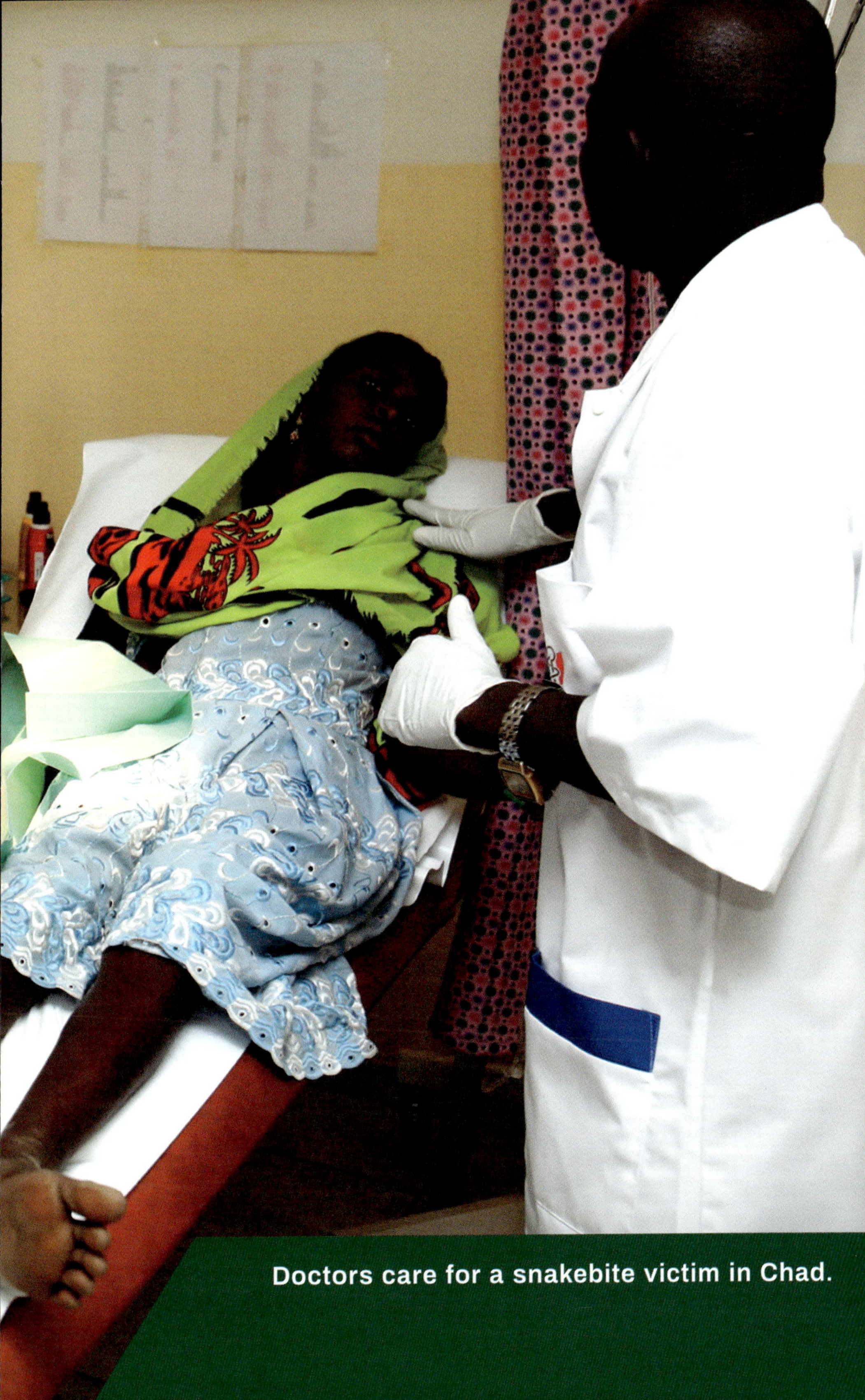

Doctors care for a snakebite victim in Chad.

A worker in Thailand milks a cobra for antivenom.

Making more antivenom is key. But it's a hard process. First, people catch snakes. Then, they "milk" the snakes. They force the snakes to bite into jars. Venom drips from the snakes' fangs into the jars. Next, people give that venom to animals. The animals' bodies respond. They create cells called antibodies. These cells fight off the venom. The cells are in part of the blood called plasma. Scientists then draw the animals' blood. They turn the plasma into antivenom.

Living in harmony with snakes is possible. In western India, some people consider snakes holy. They believe killing snakes brings bad fortune. This is good for snakes. People want to protect them. People create special groves. Snakes are left alone there. This helps cut down on snake attacks.

INDIA'S SNAKE CATCHERS

The Irulas are an Indigenous people in South India. They are known for catching snakes. They get venom from the snakes they catch. This venom helps make antivenom. India's biggest supply of venom comes from the Irulas.

Some people learn how to perform with snakes. They are known as snake charmers.

A rattlesnake shakes its tail as a warning.

Most bites happen when people try to hold snakes. So, staying away from snakes can help. So can watching carefully. Snakes often give warnings before they strike. They may rattle or hiss. Others will try to slither away. If snakes do this, people should leave them alone.

SAVING LIVES

In 2022, someone in Indiana was bitten by a deadly snake. The hospital called the Toledo Zoo in Ohio. The zoo had the right antivenom. Police raced to the zoo for the antivenom. Then they drove hundreds of miles to Indiana. They saved the victim's life.

MAP

1. Tennessee, United States: A copperhead hides in a baby stroller.
2. Valle del Cauca, Colombia: A man is hospitalized after a bite from a fer-de-lance.
3. Ohio, United States: The Toledo Zoo provides lifesaving antivenom to a snakebite victim.

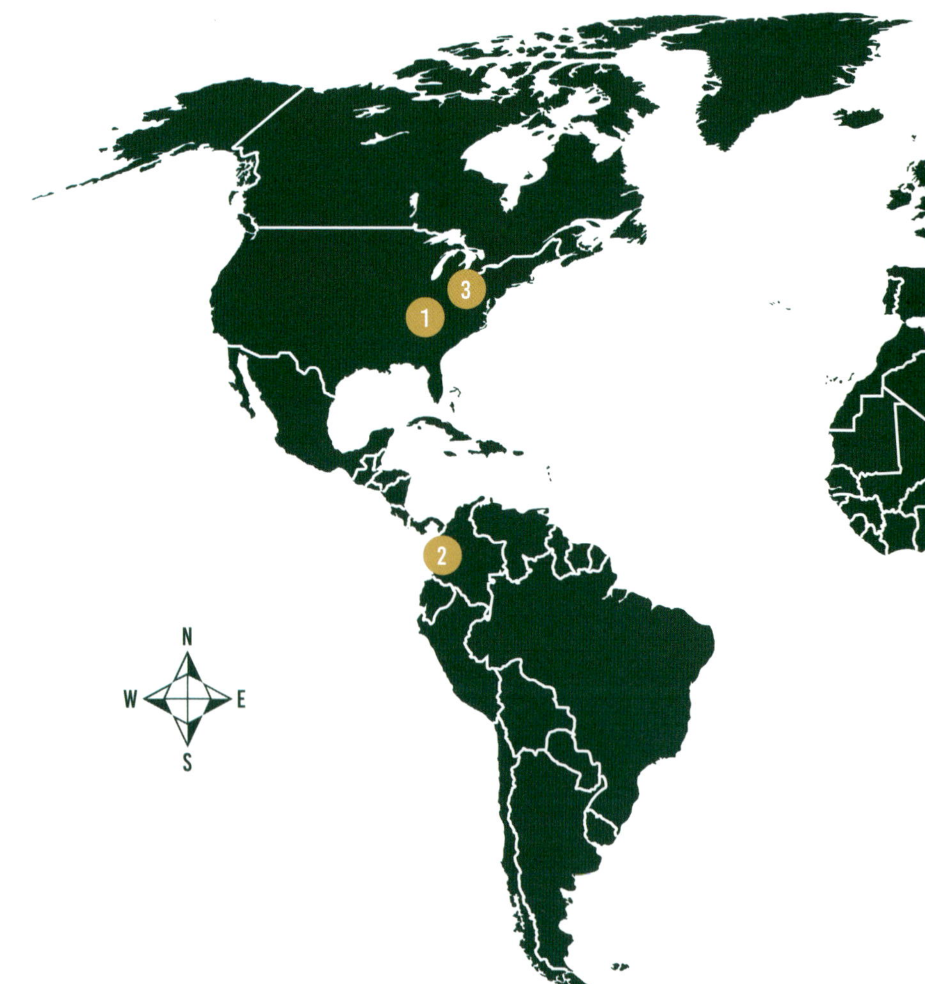

4 Equator, Democratic Republic of the Congo: A fisher dies from a snakebite before he reaches the hospital.

5 Western Cape, South Africa: A snouted cobra bites a man during an antivenom shortage.

6 Tamil Nadu, India: Irula snake catchers produce the country's largest supply of venom for antivenom.

7 Great Barrier Reef, Australia: Sea snakes attack divers.

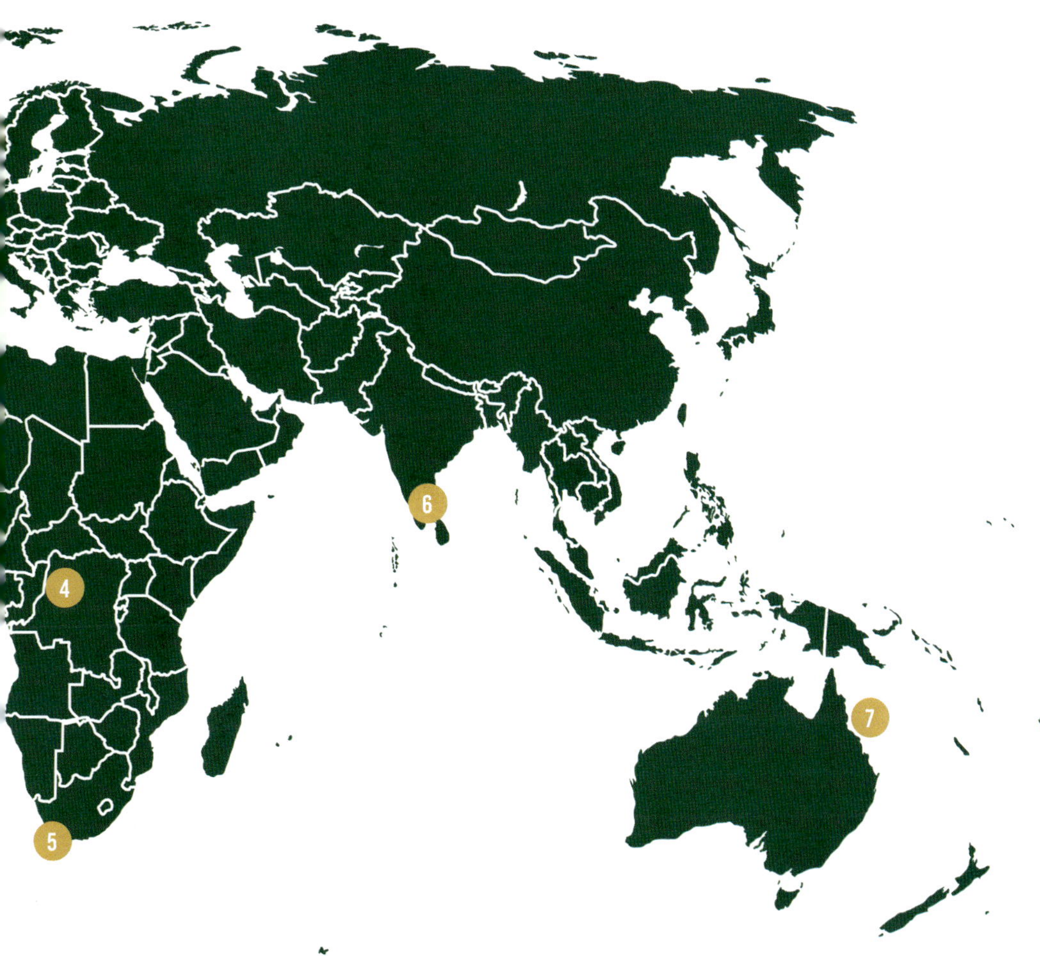

COMPREHENSION QUESTIONS

Write your answers on a separate piece of paper.

1. Write a paragraph explaining the main ideas of Chapter 6.

2. Would you want to see a deadly snake? Why or why not?

3. Which snake is one of the Big Four in India?

   A. inland taipan
   B. rattlesnake
   C. common krait

4. How does sensing heat help pit vipers find prey?

   A. Pit vipers live in cold places.
   B. Animals give off body heat.
   C. Pit vipers don't have eyes.

5. What does **behavior** mean in this book?

Snake ***behavior*** *is key, too. Some snakes hide from people. Others tend to attack if they feel threatened.*

A. where animals live
B. what animals look like
C. how animals act

6. What does **constrictors** mean in this book?

They don't use venom. Instead, they are ***constrictors****. They kill by squeezing their prey.*

A. snakes that kill by wrapping tightly
B. snakes that kill with venom
C. snakes that do not kill other animals

Answer key on page 64.

GLOSSARY

aggressive
Strong and quick to attack.

antivenom
Medicine that stops the harm of venom.

camouflage
Colors or markings that help animals blend in with the area around them.

Indigenous
Related to the original people who lived in an area.

invasive
Spreading quickly in a new area and causing many problems there.

mammals
Animals that have hair and produce milk for their young.

monsoon
A strong wind that causes a season of very wet or dry weather in an area.

nervous system
The body's system of long, thin fibers called nerves. Nerves carry information between the brain and other parts of the body.

paralyzes
Makes something unable to move.

venom
A harmful substance made by an animal and used to bite or sting prey.

TO LEARN MORE

BOOKS

Beer, Julie. *Bite, Sting, Kill! The Incredible Science of Toxins, Venom, Fangs & Stingers*. Washington, DC: National Geographic Kids, 2023.

Downs, Kieran. *King Cobra vs. Mongoose*. Minneapolis: Bellwether Media, 2022.

Huddleston, Emma. *Burmese Pythons*. Mendota Heights, MN: Focus Readers, 2022.

ONLINE RESOURCES

Visit **www.apexeditions.com** to find links and resources related to this title.

ABOUT THE AUTHOR

Kathleen Reitmann grew up in New York and has an MS in education. She also has an MS in nursing from DePaul University in Chicago, Illinois. Katheen is the author of 26 classroom books for children. She is a nurse by day and a writer by night.

INDEX

ANSWER KEY:

1. Answers will vary; 2. Answers will vary; 3. C; 4. B; 5. C; 6. A